Who Am I?

by

Giora Carmi

This book does not have a copyright.
Please use it as you wish.

Then sink into your honest place and see: Isn't the way you use the book another attempt at answering the question on the cover?

Next to every drawing there is an empty page. It is for you. All is possible.

And in the end, please know that none of the drawings gives the answer.

So who are you?

Do you think I know the answer?

Ha!

the beginning of 2020. New York City.
Giora Carmi
giora.carmi@**gmail**.com
gioracarmi.com

ISBN: 9798604875100

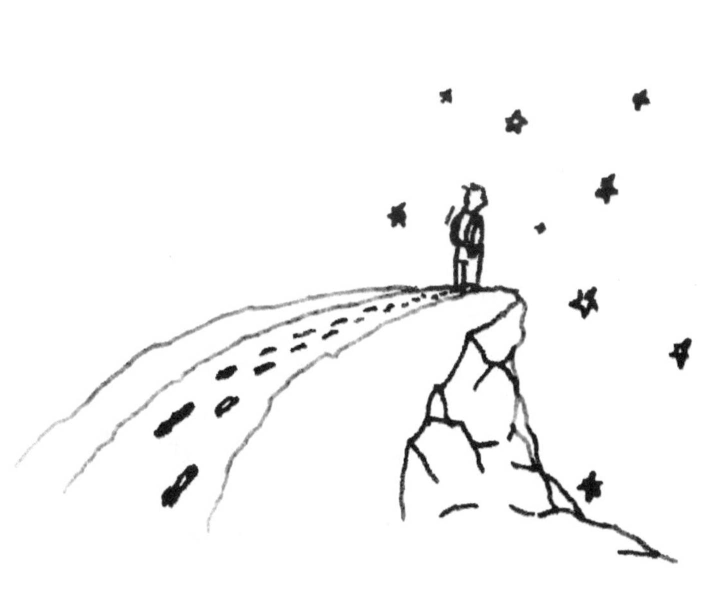

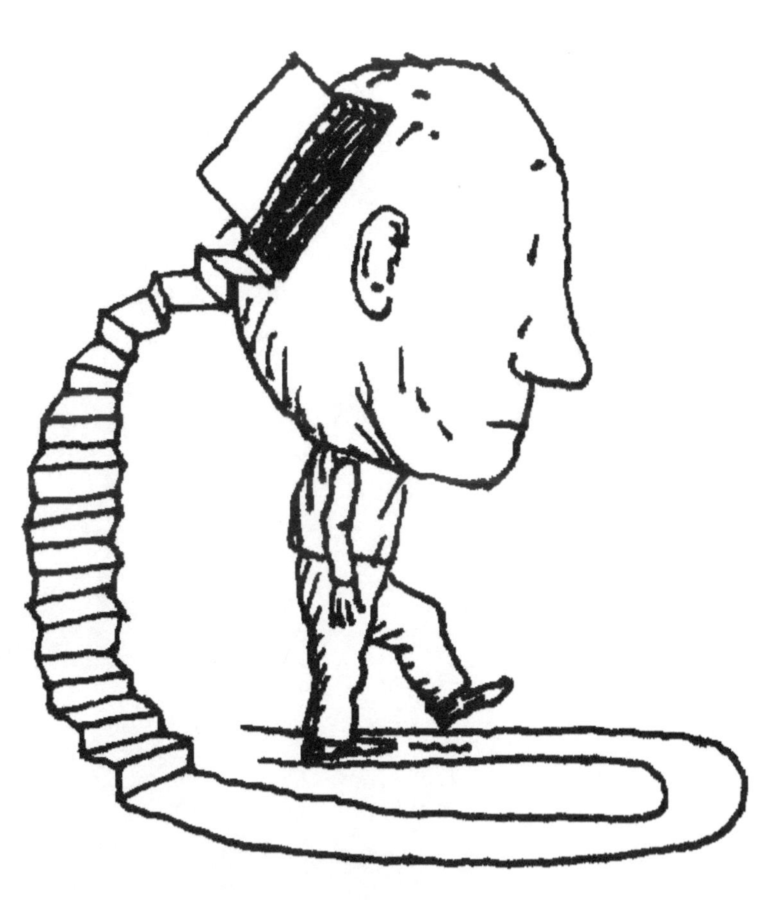

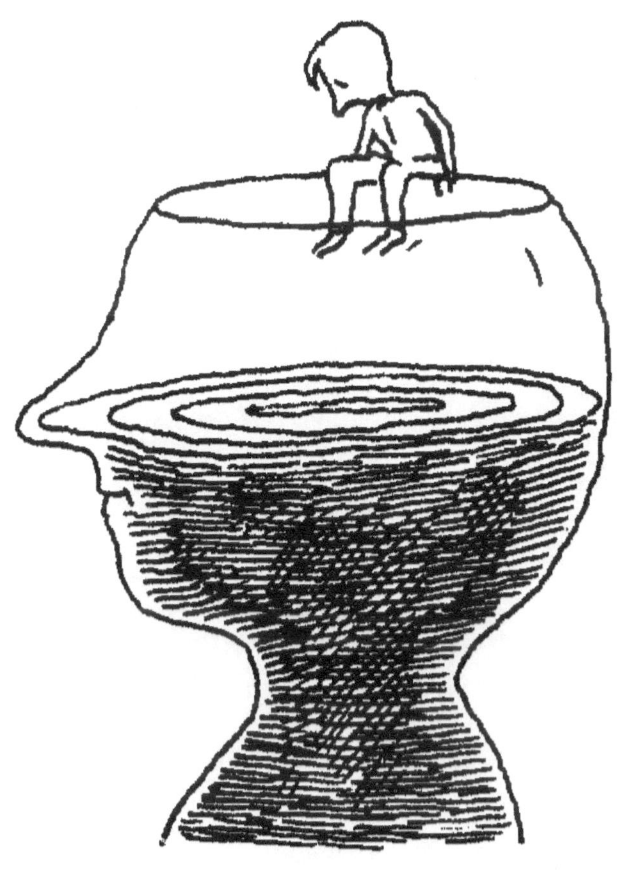

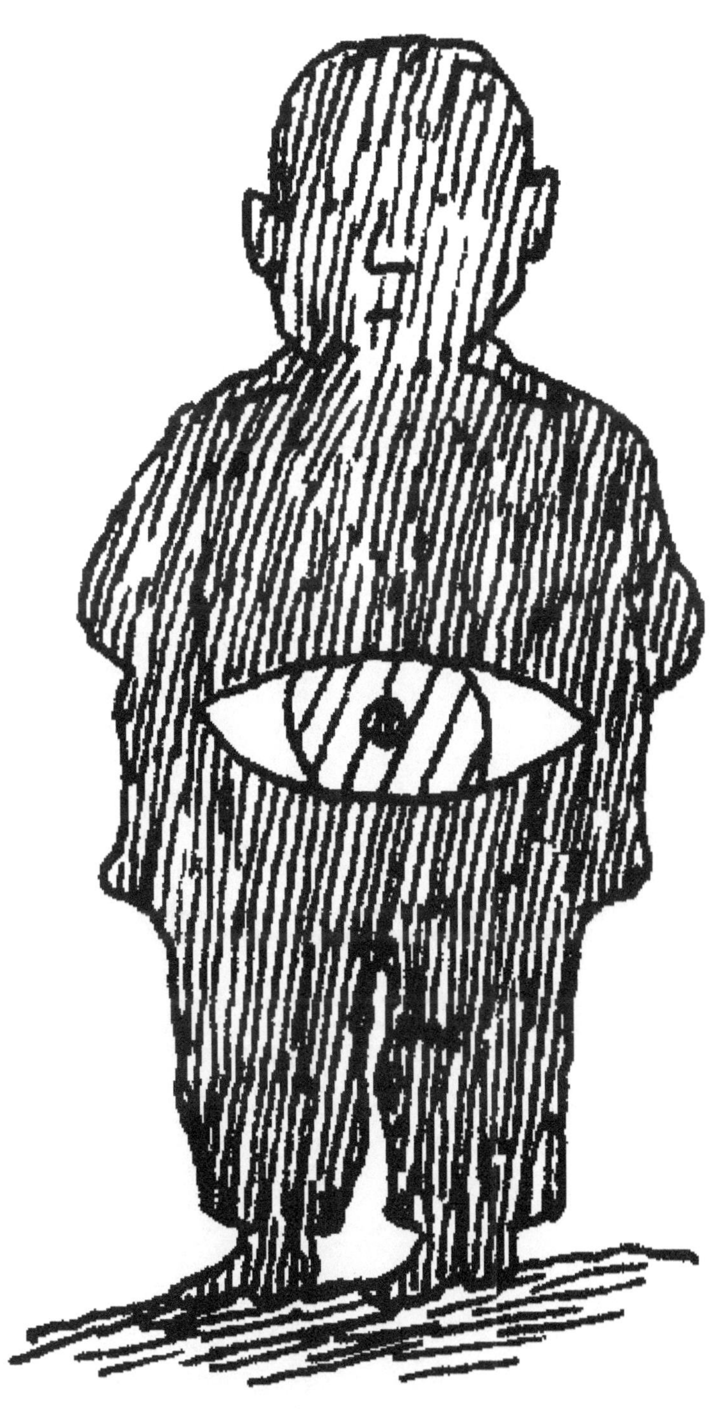

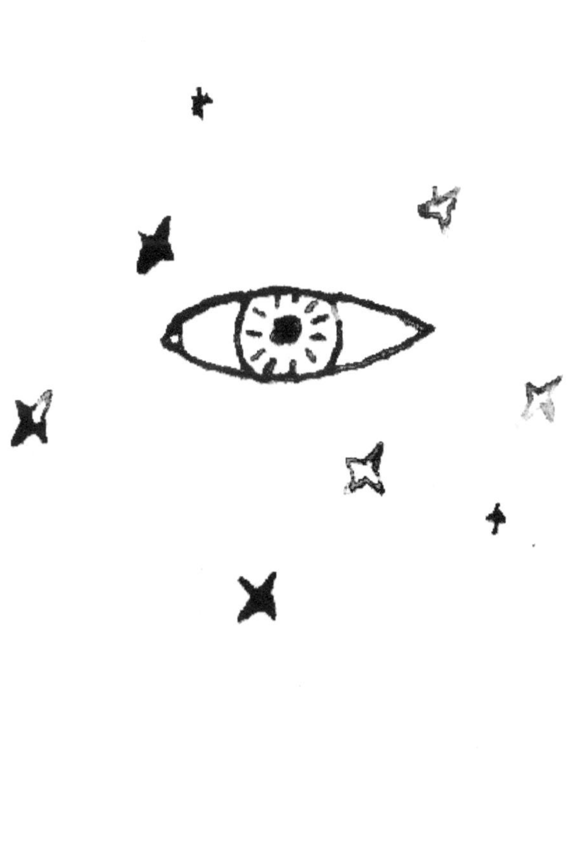

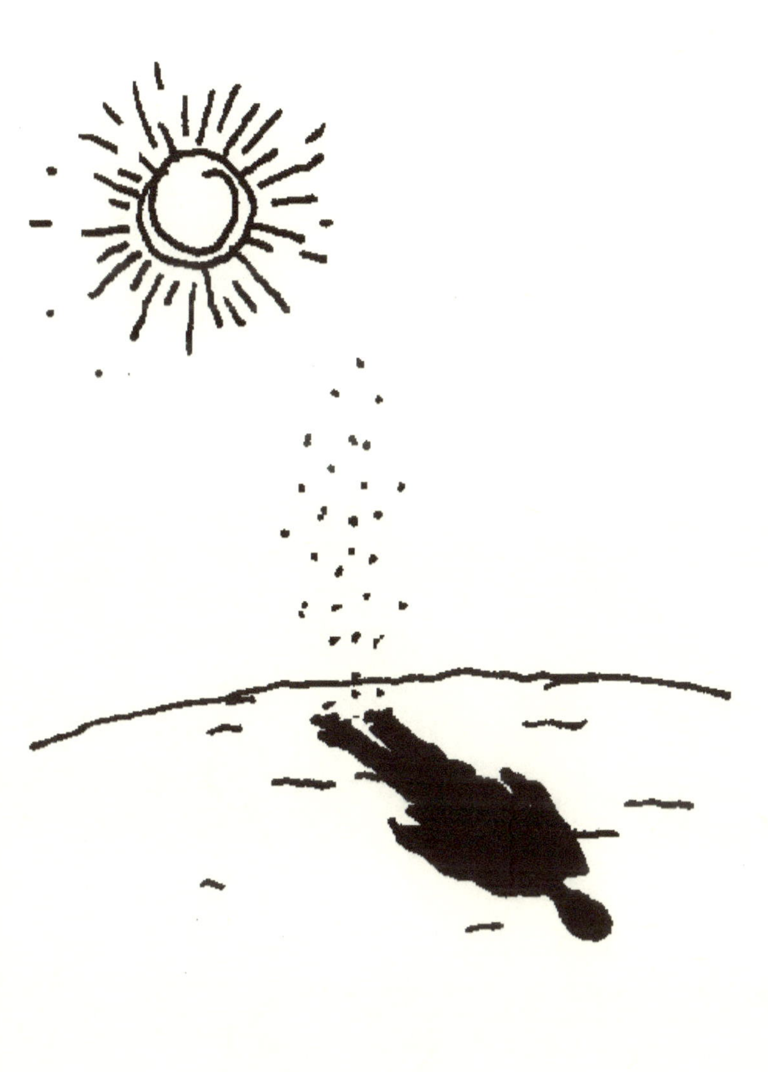

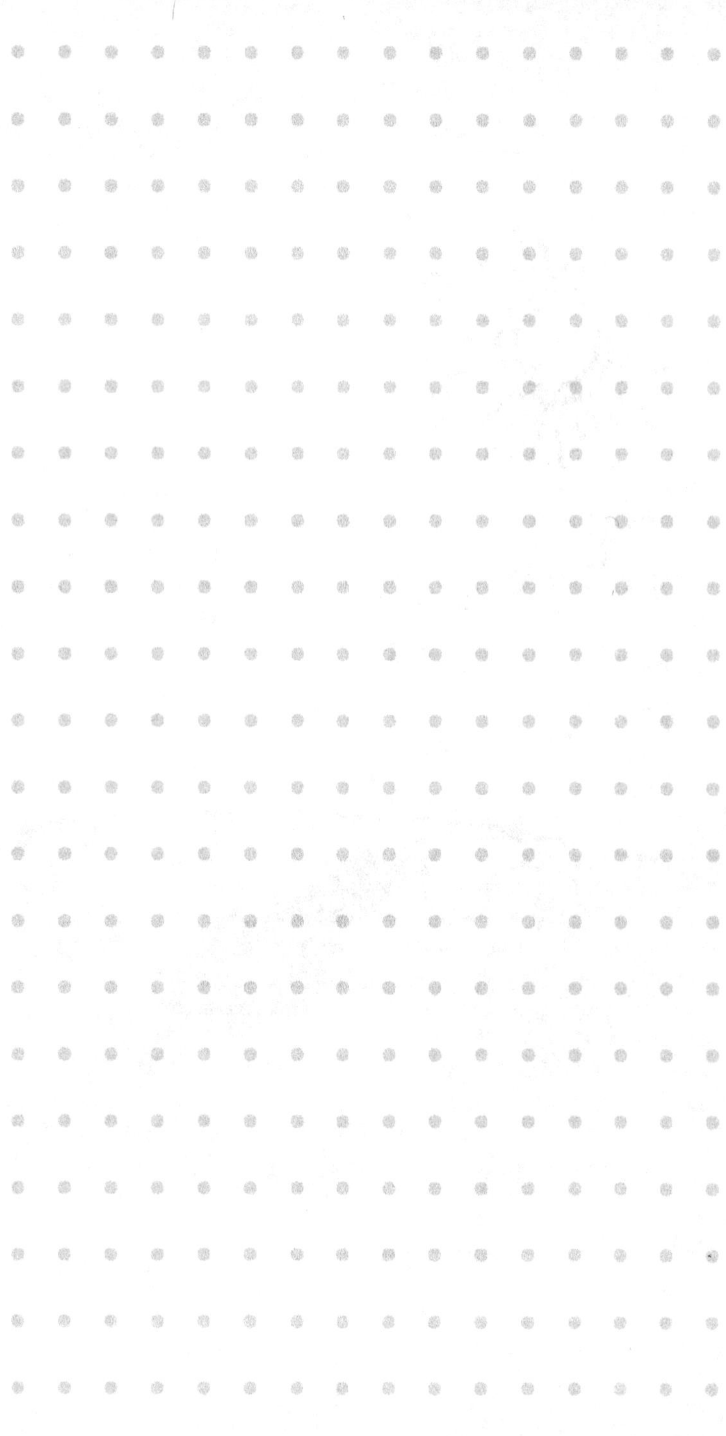

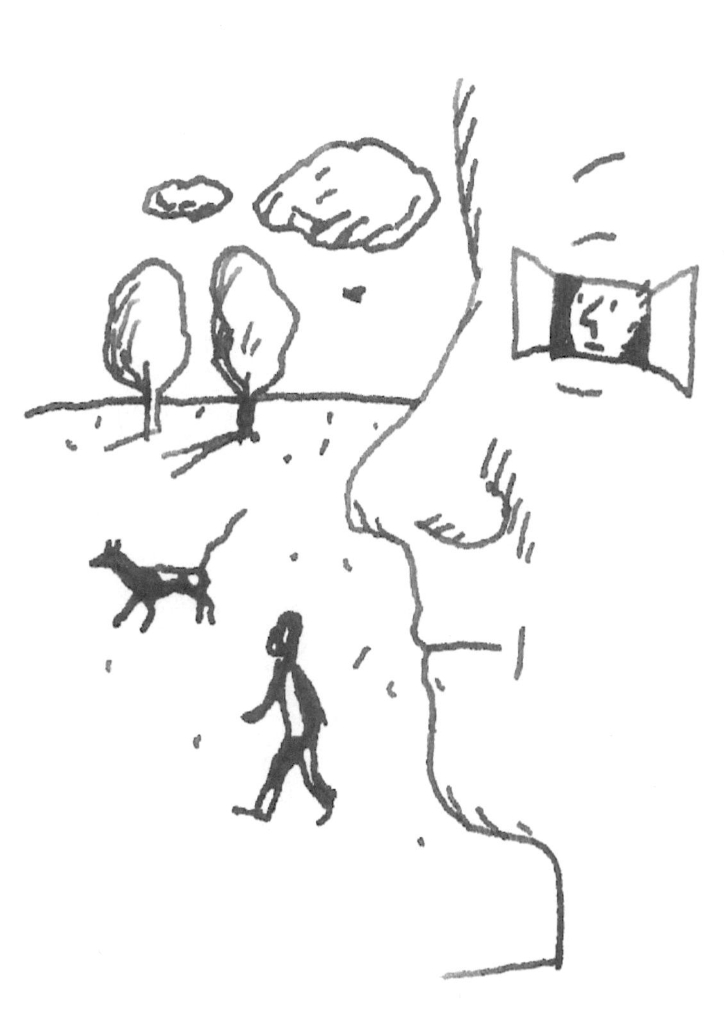

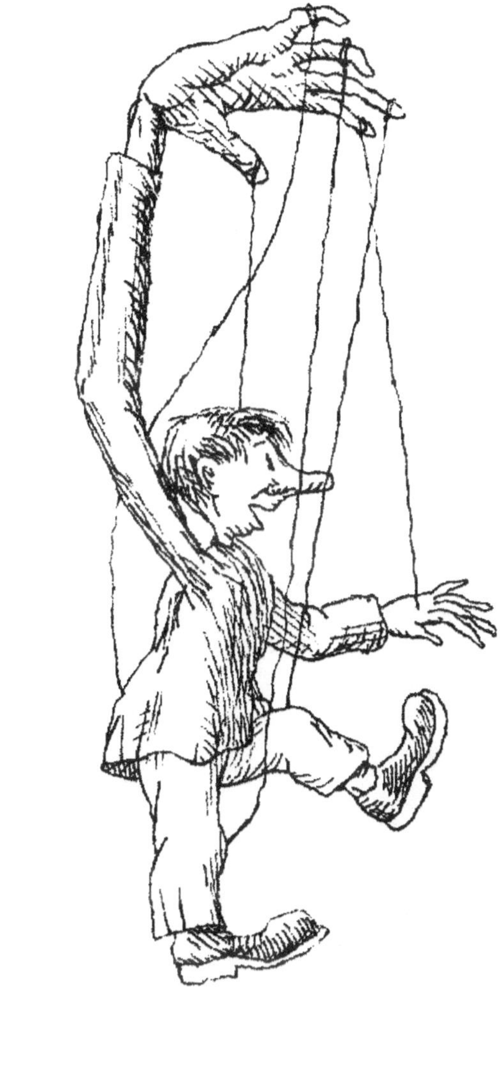

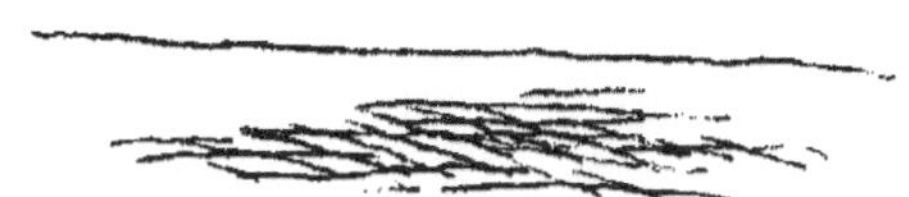

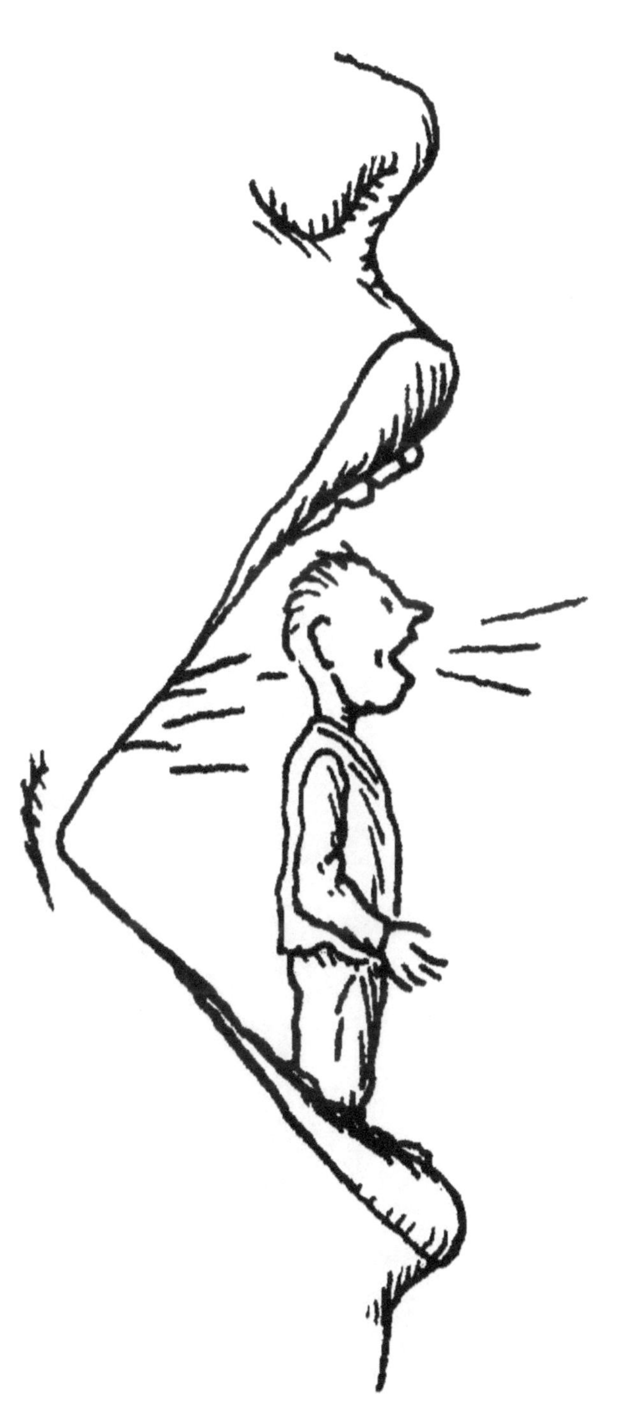

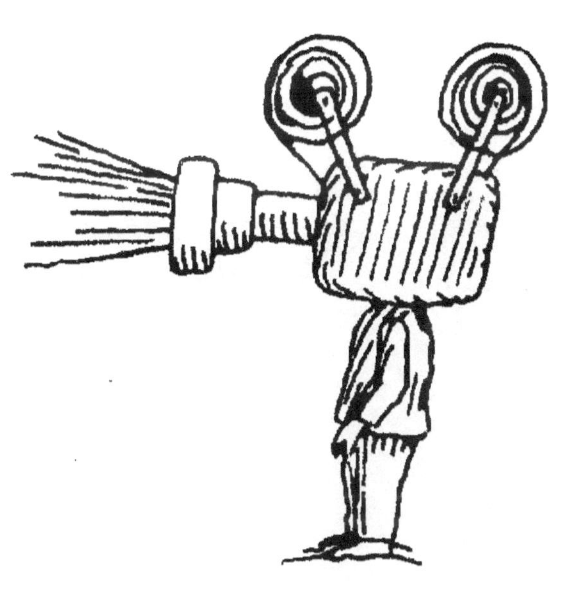

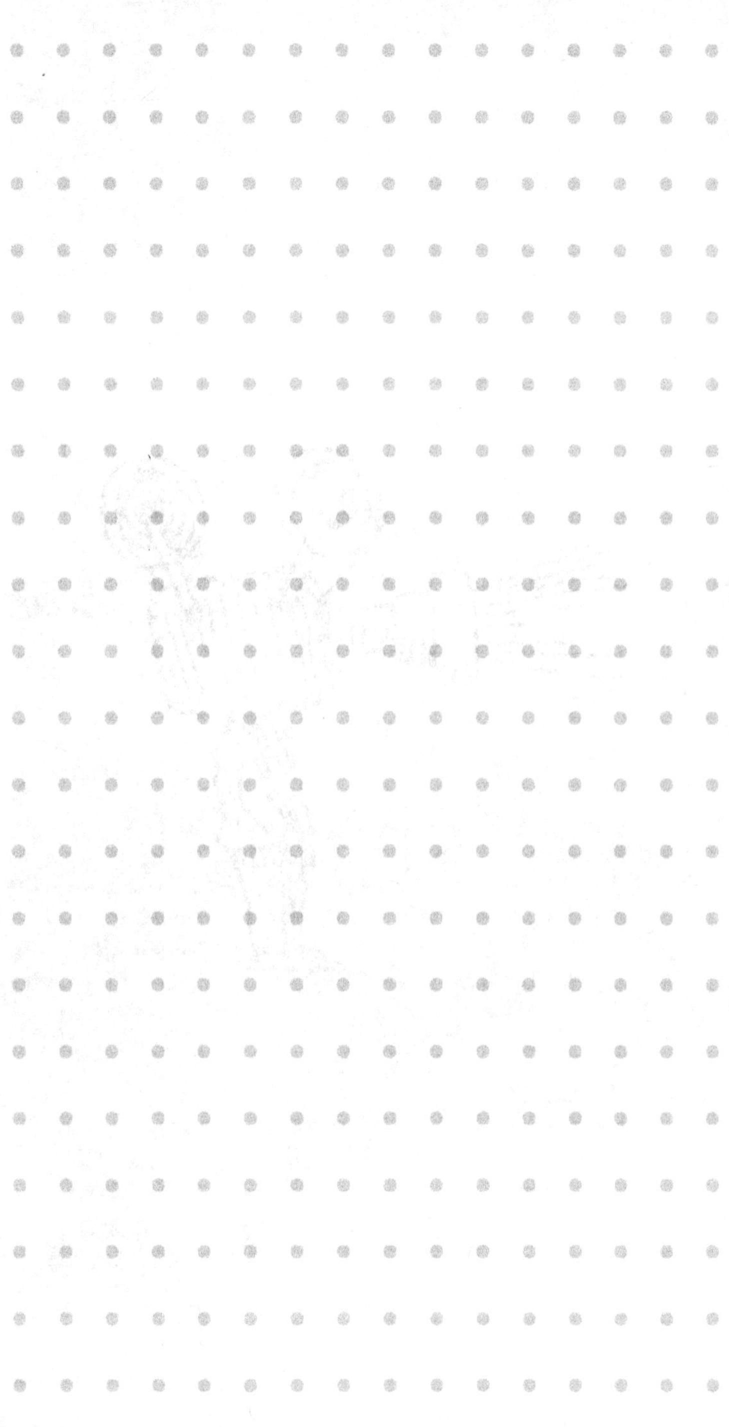

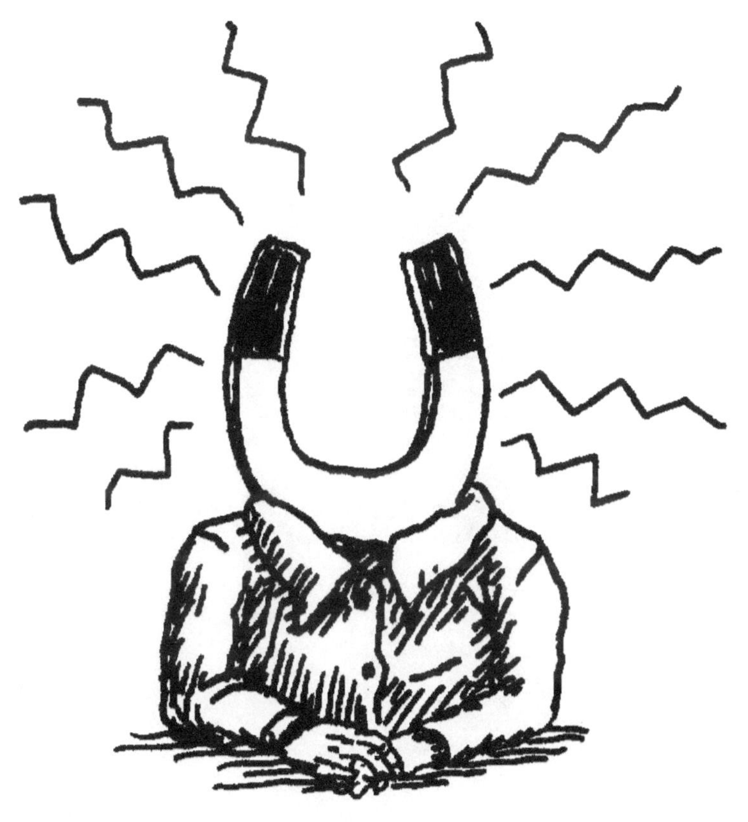

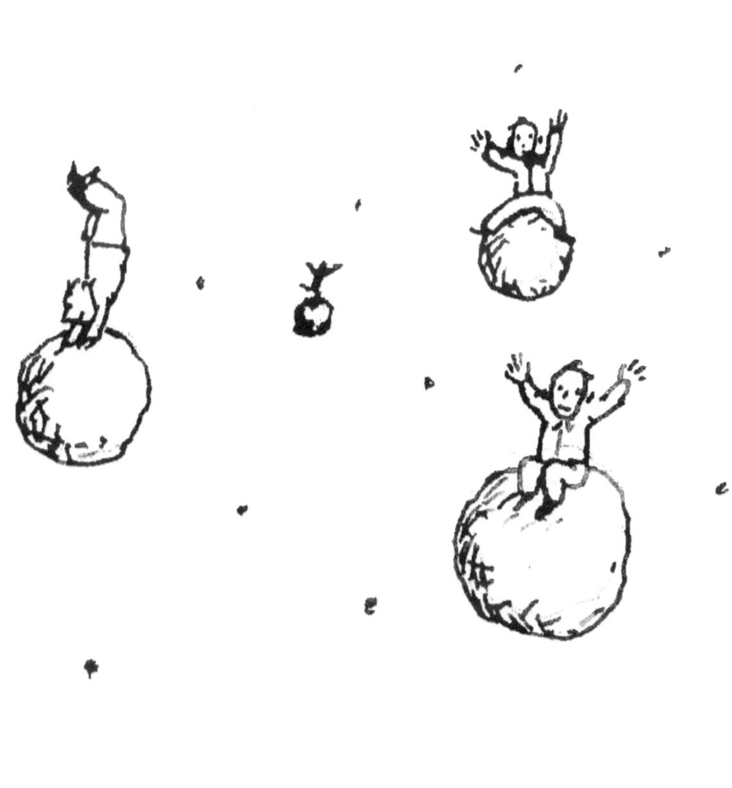

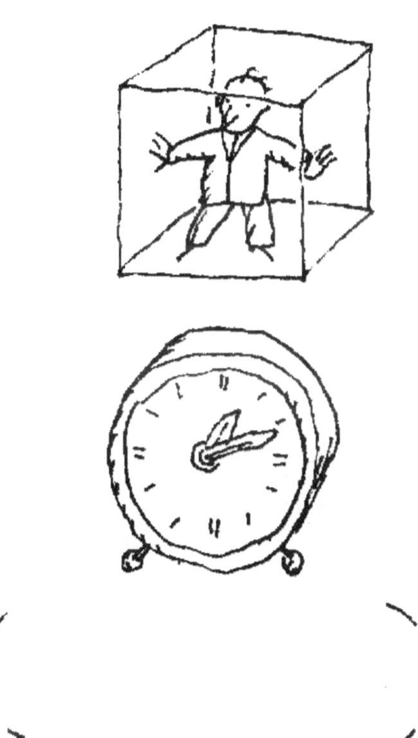

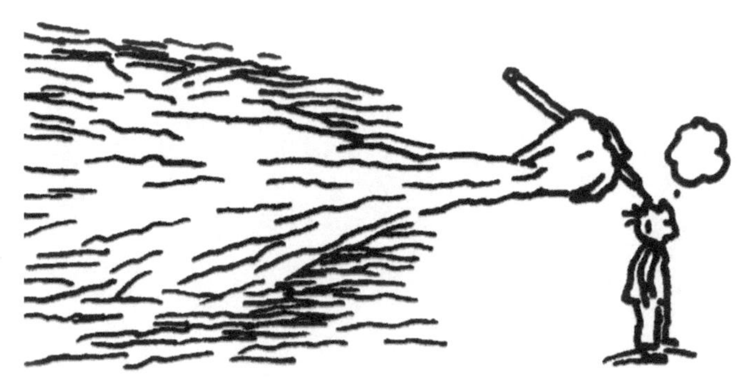

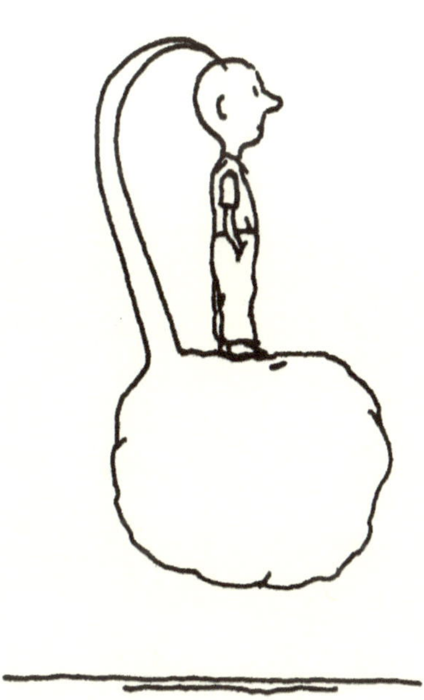

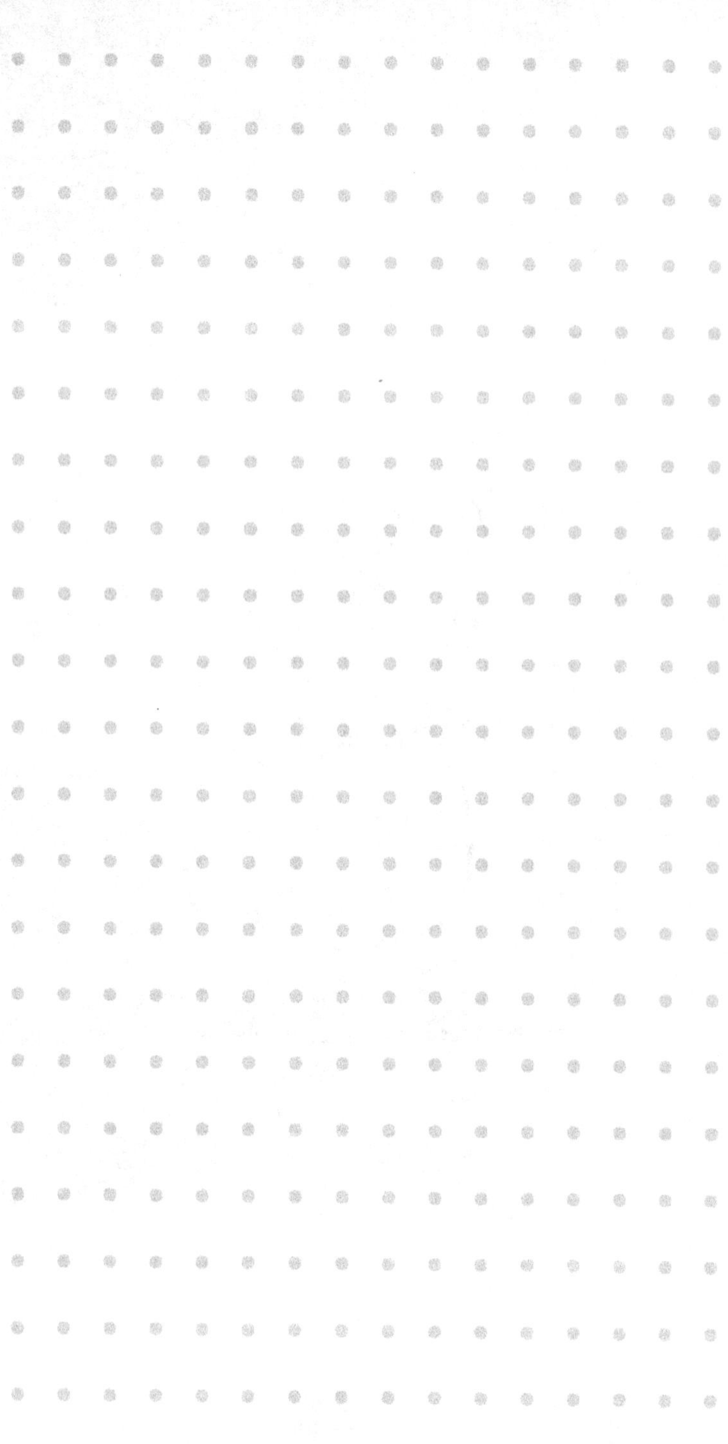

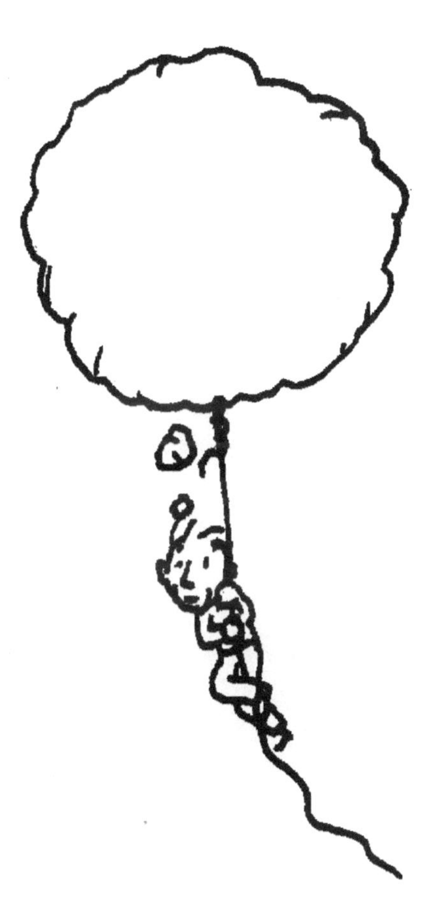

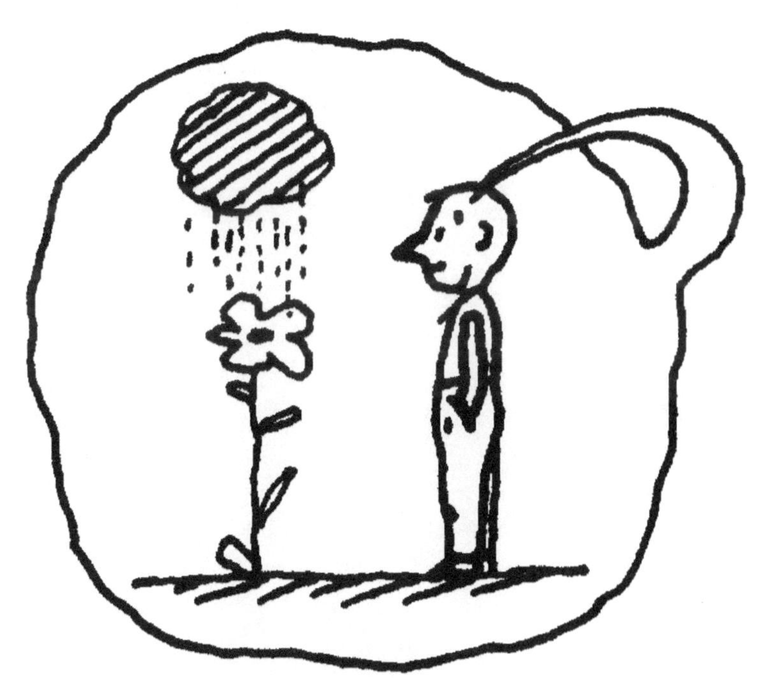

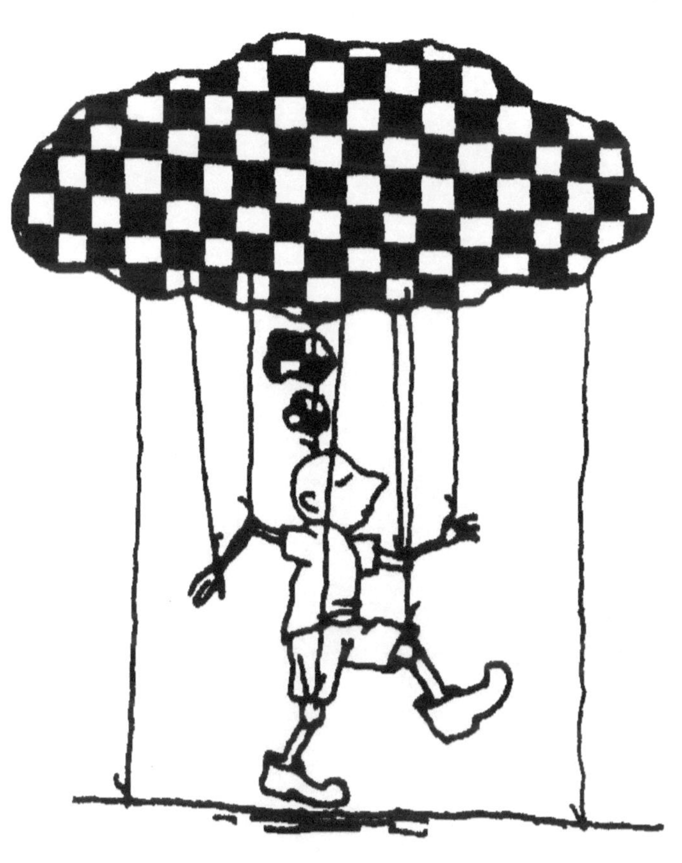

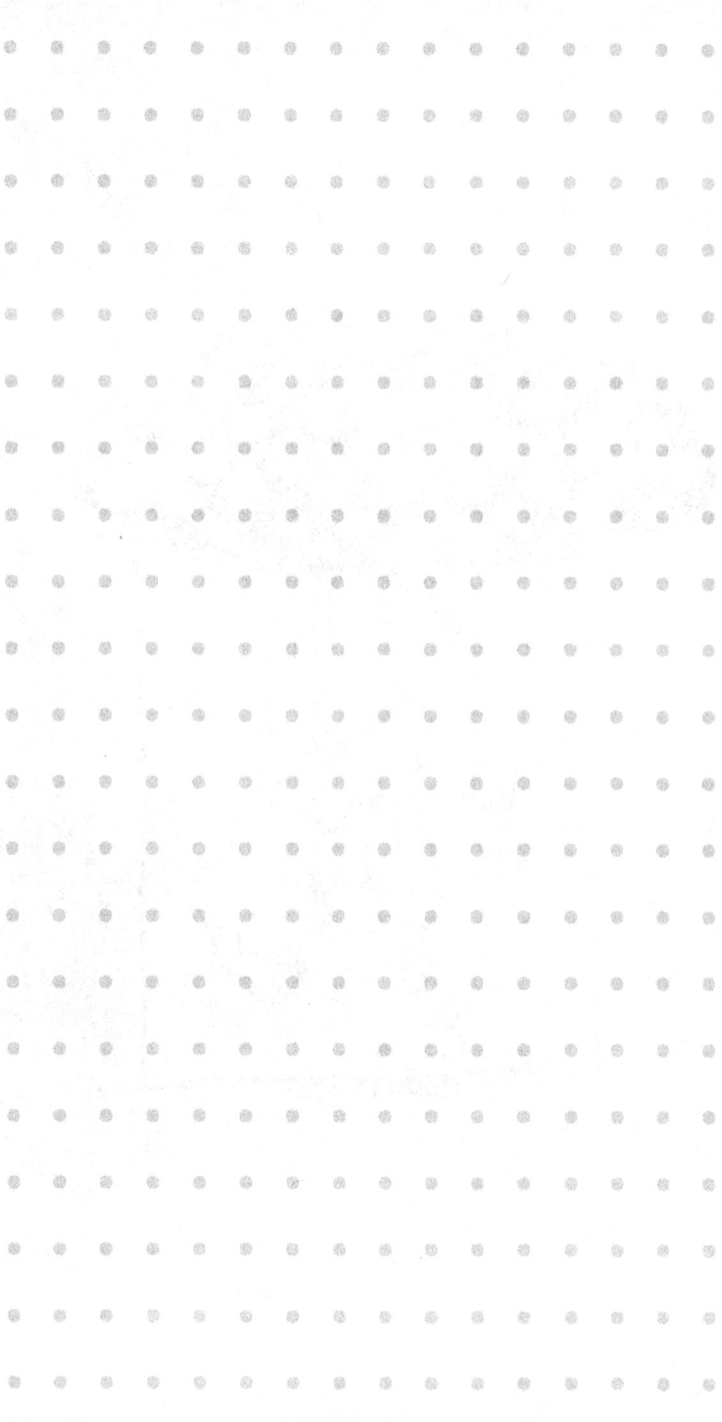

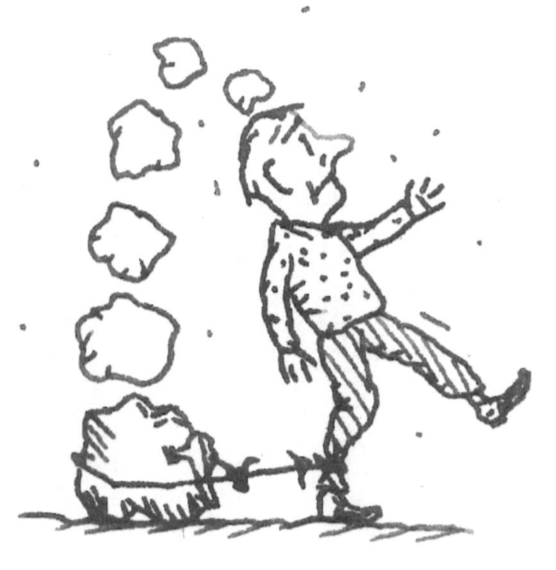

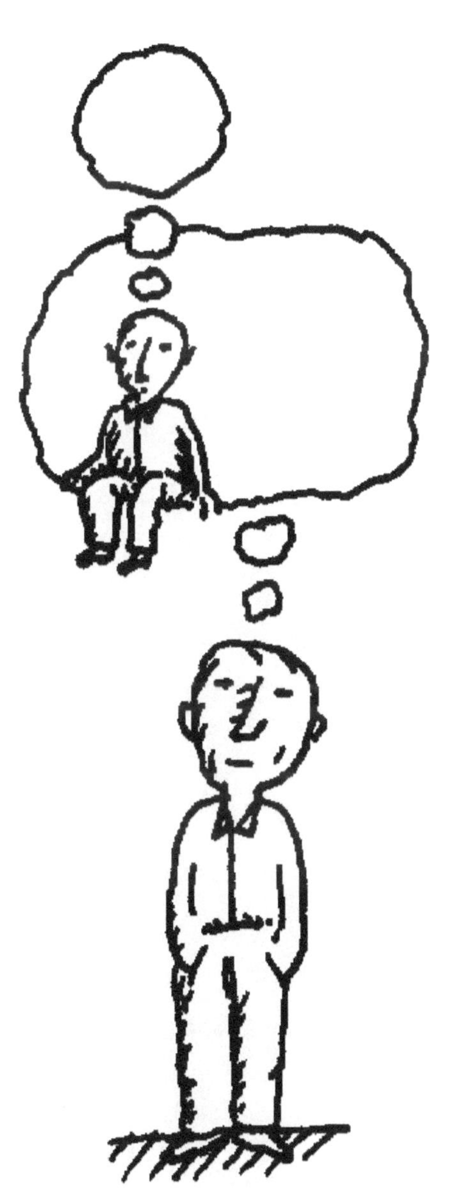

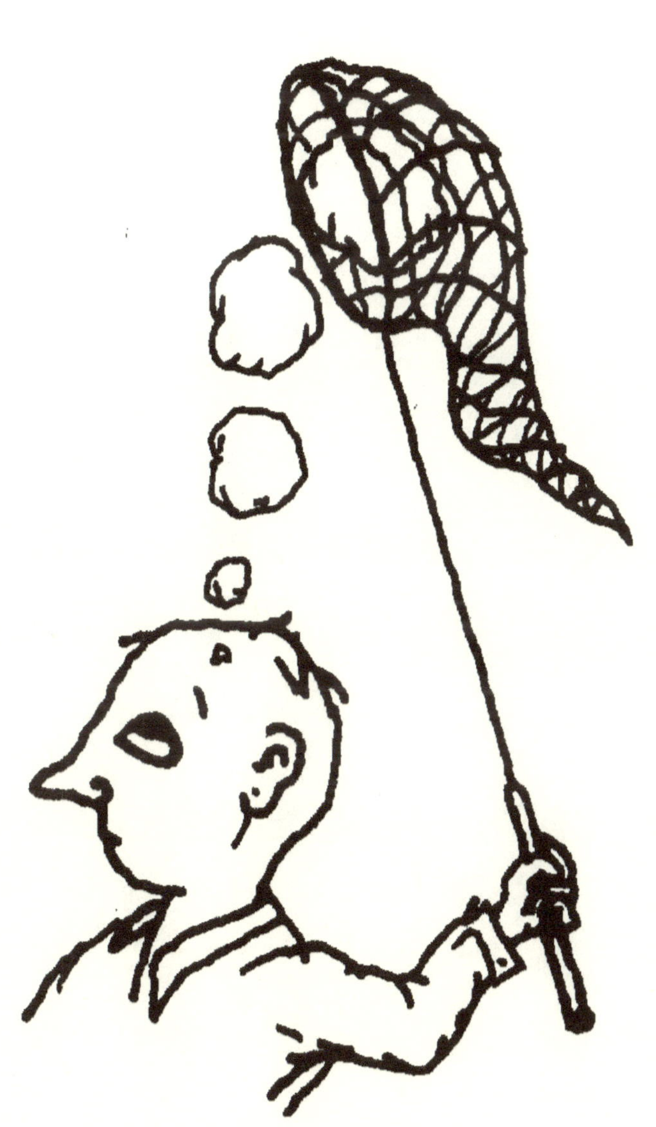

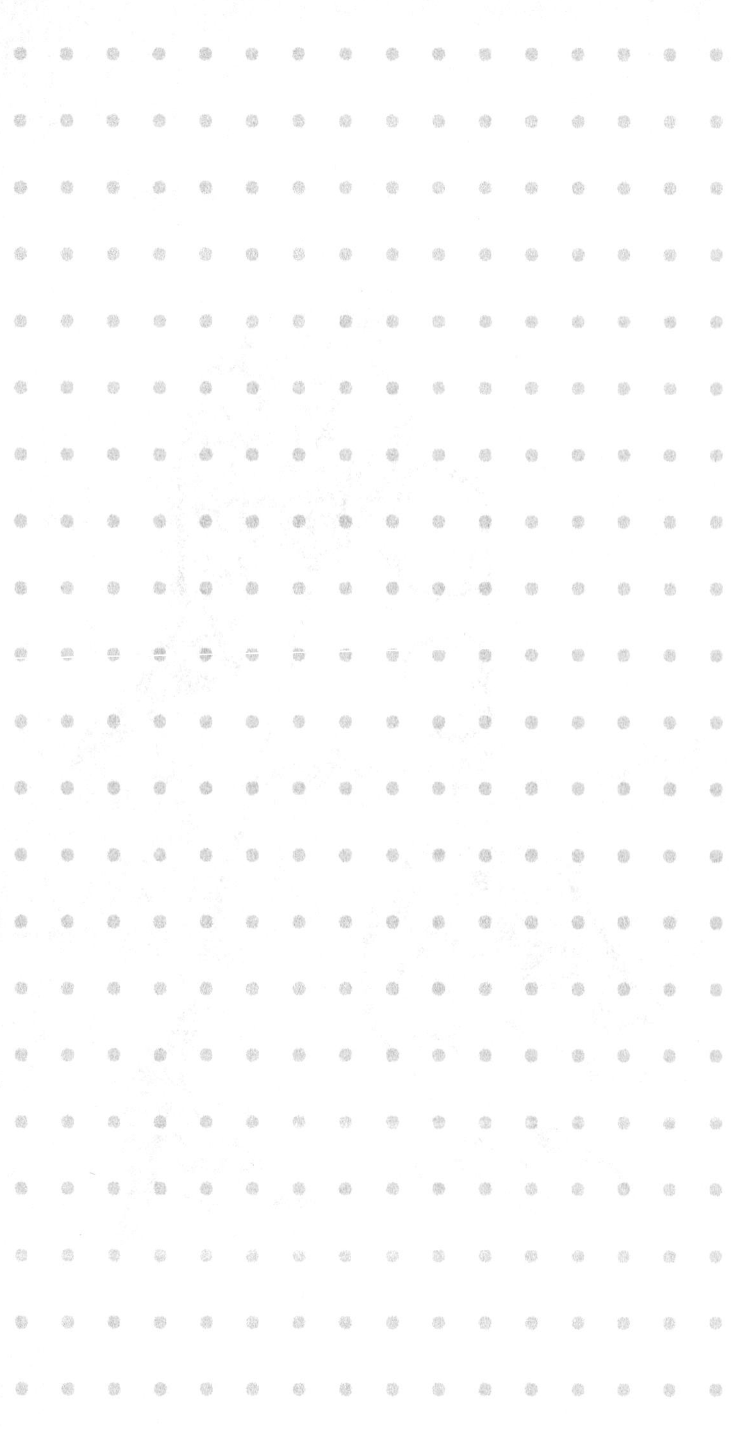

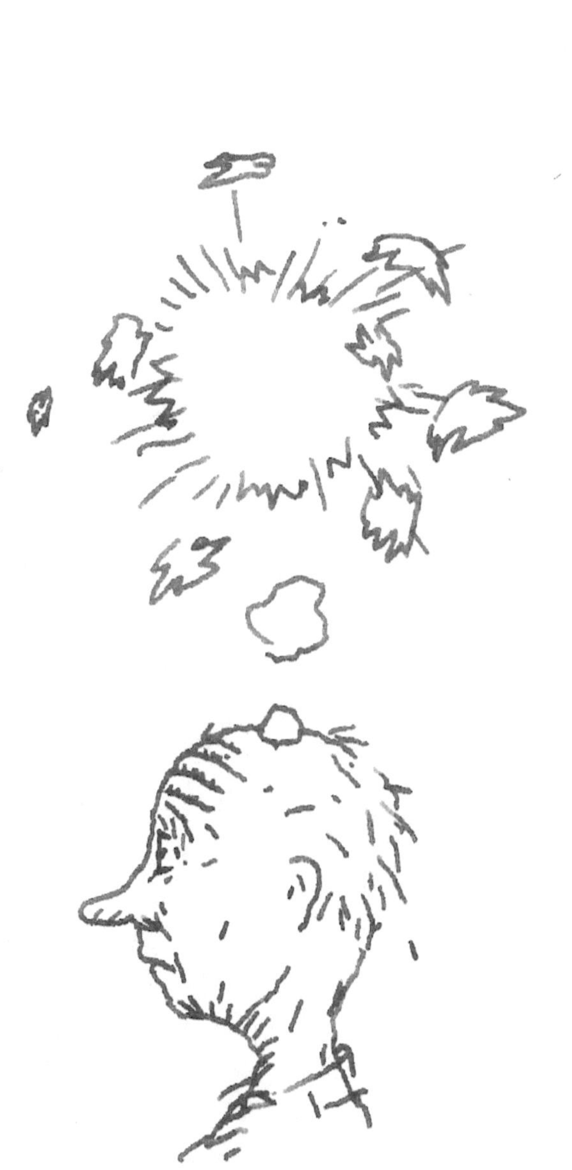

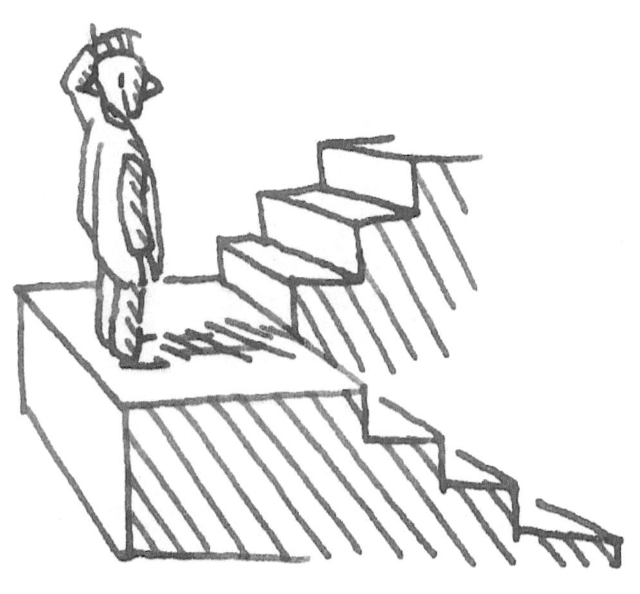

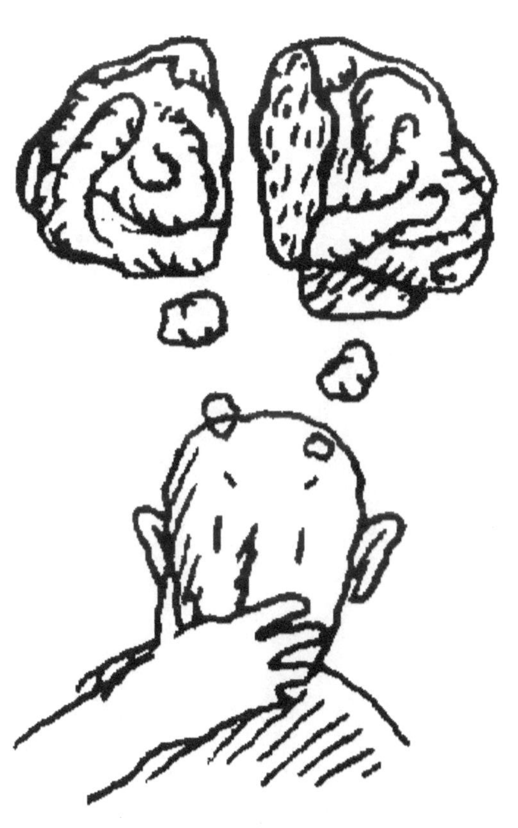

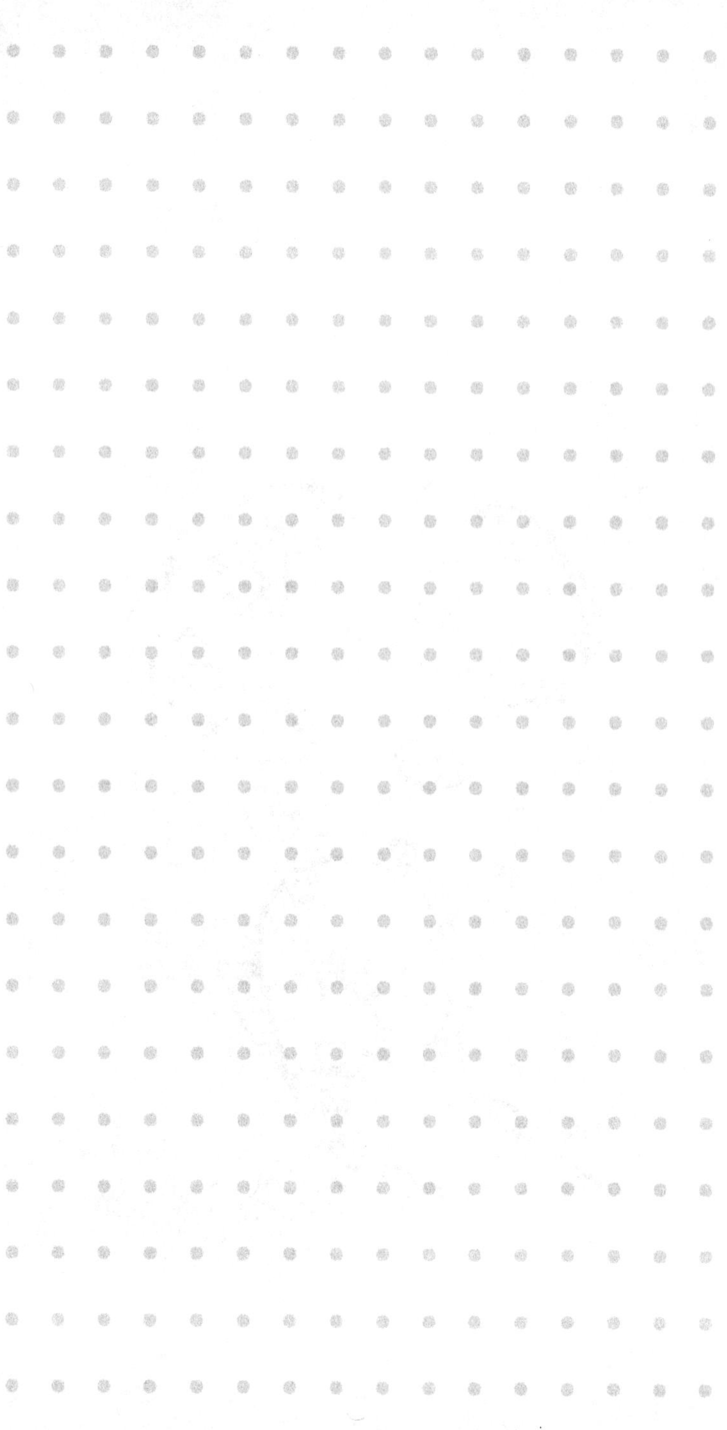

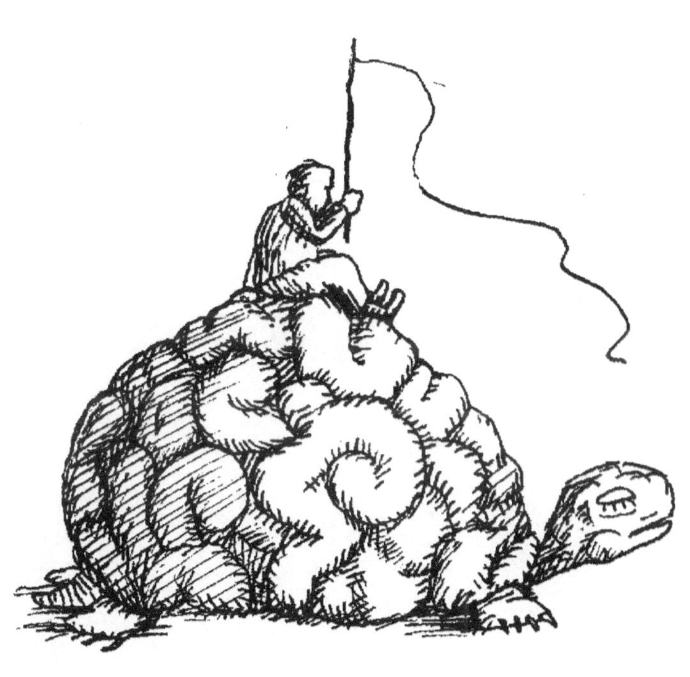

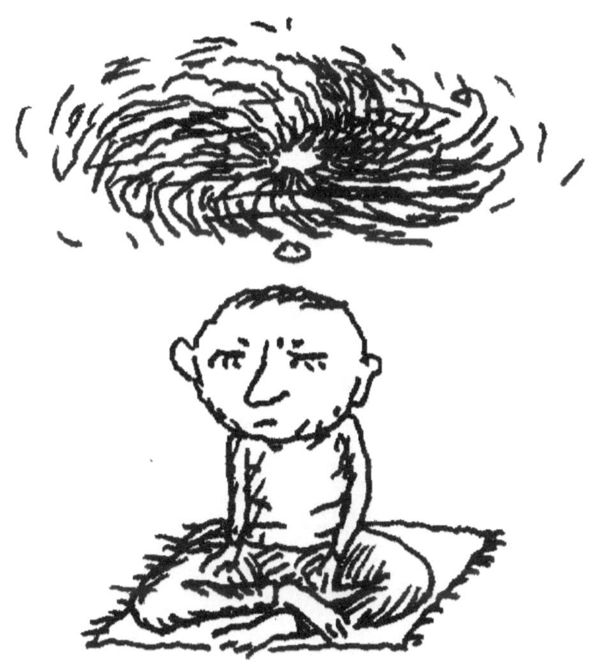

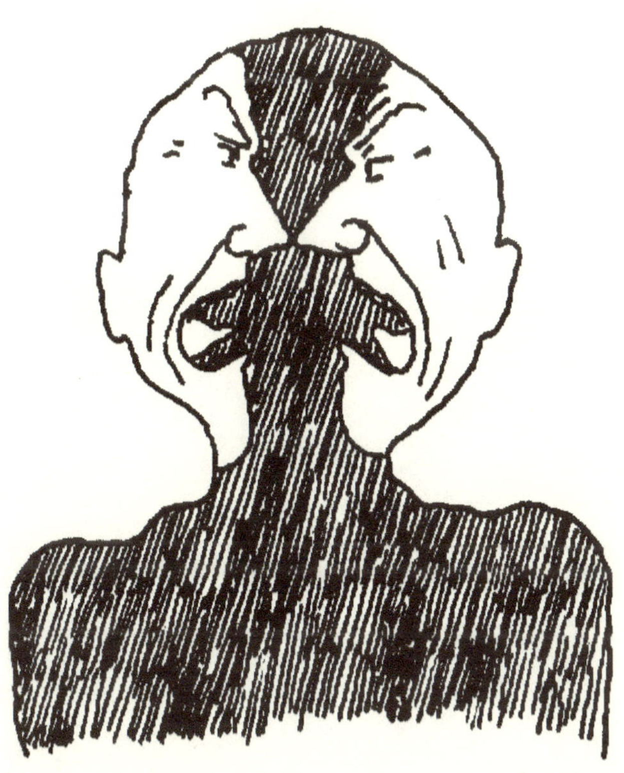

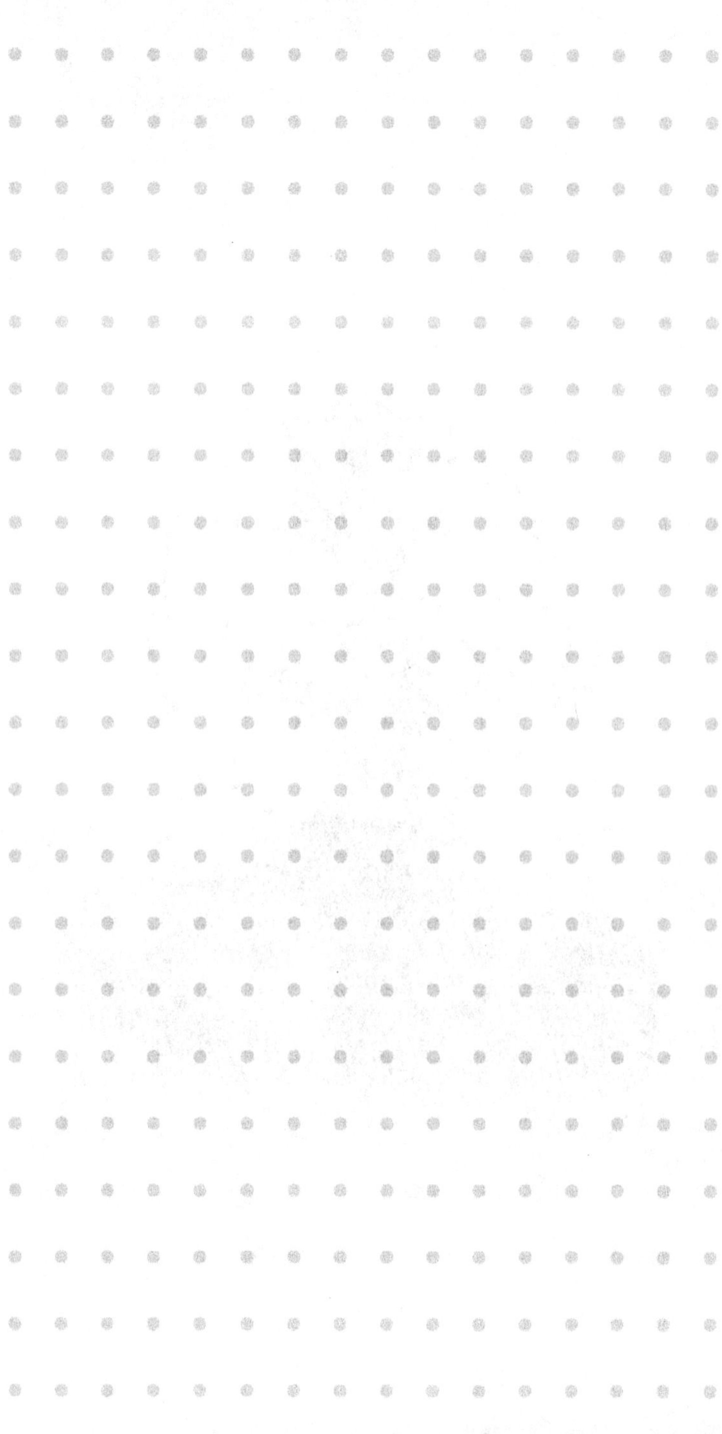

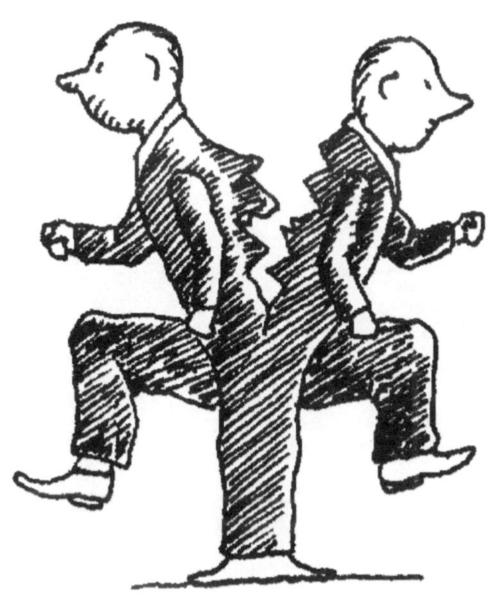

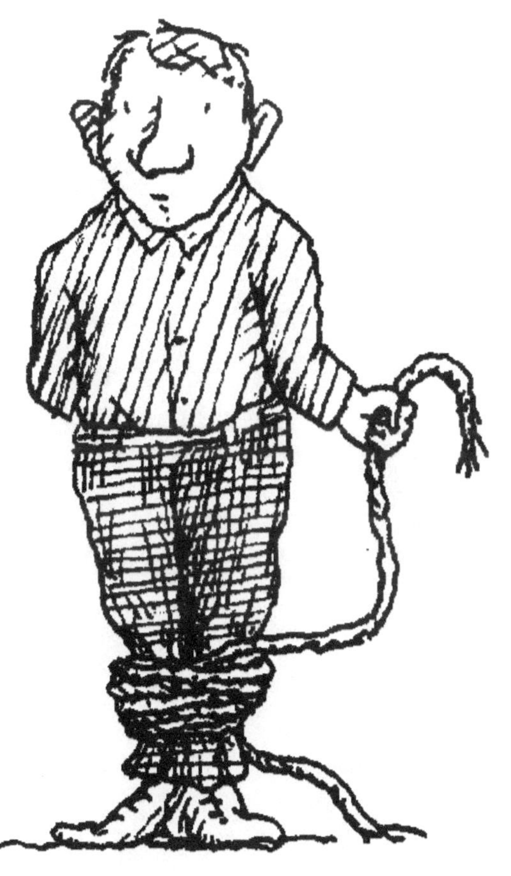

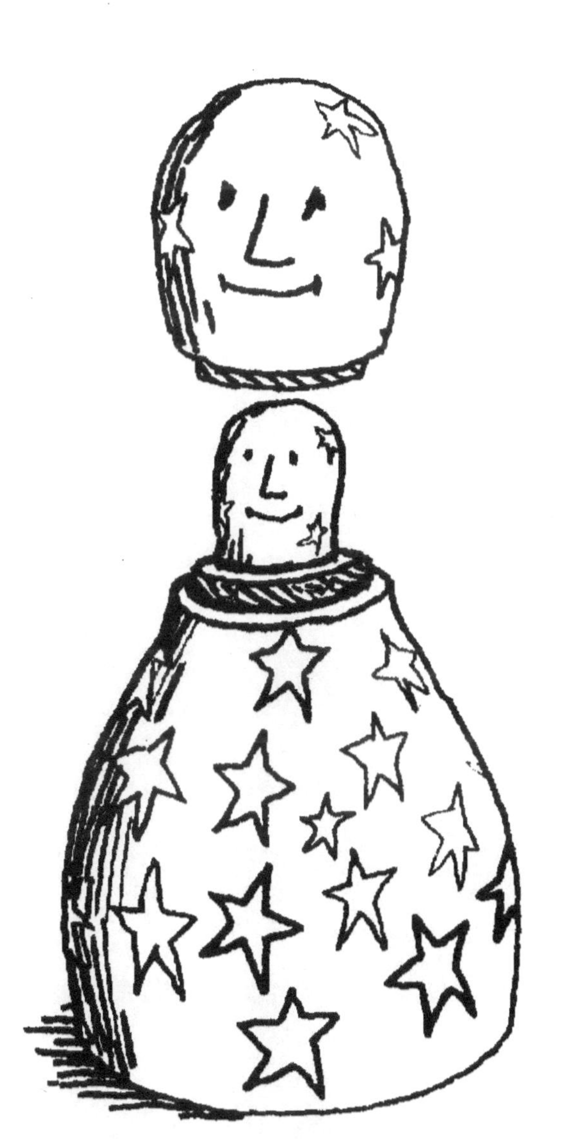

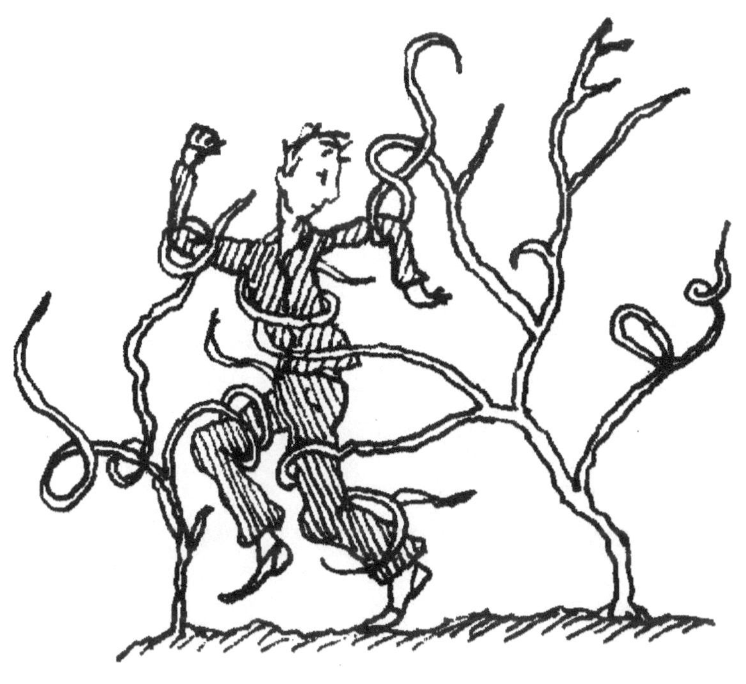

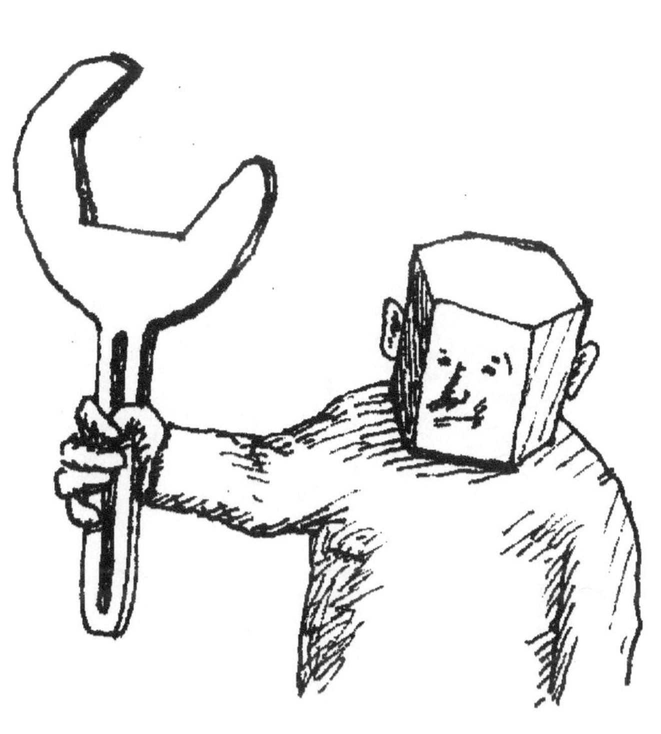

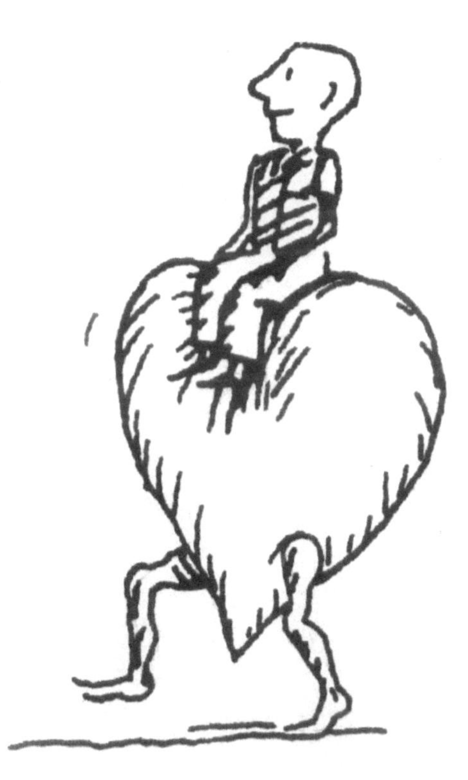

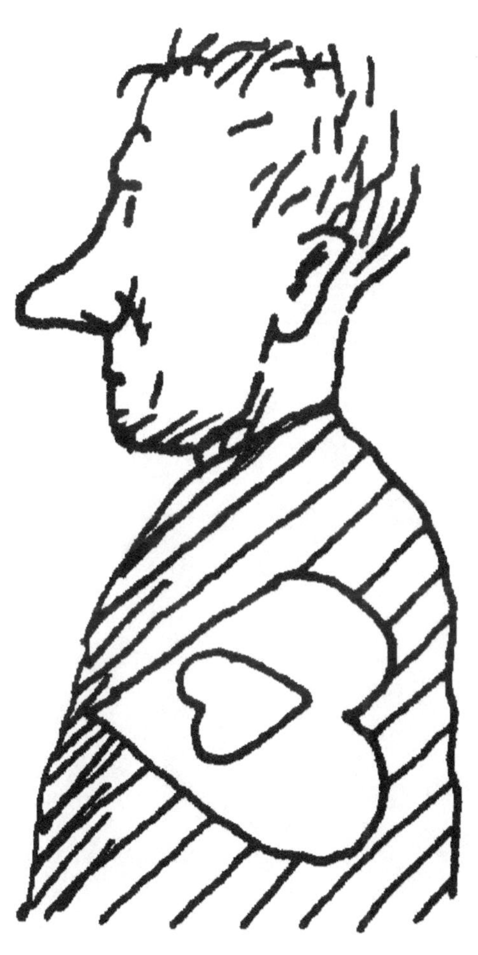

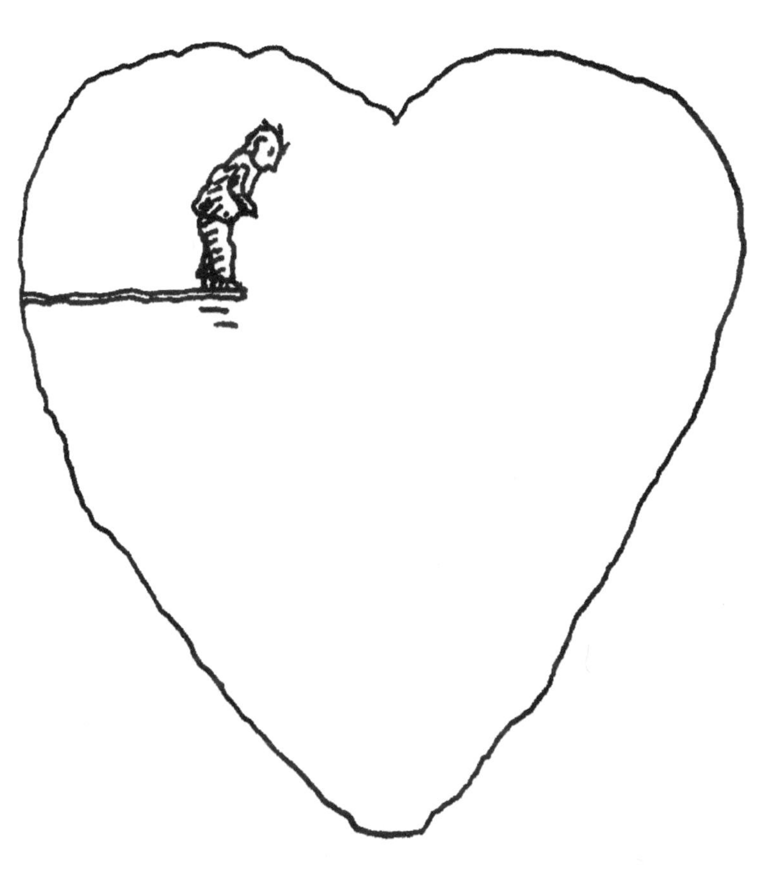

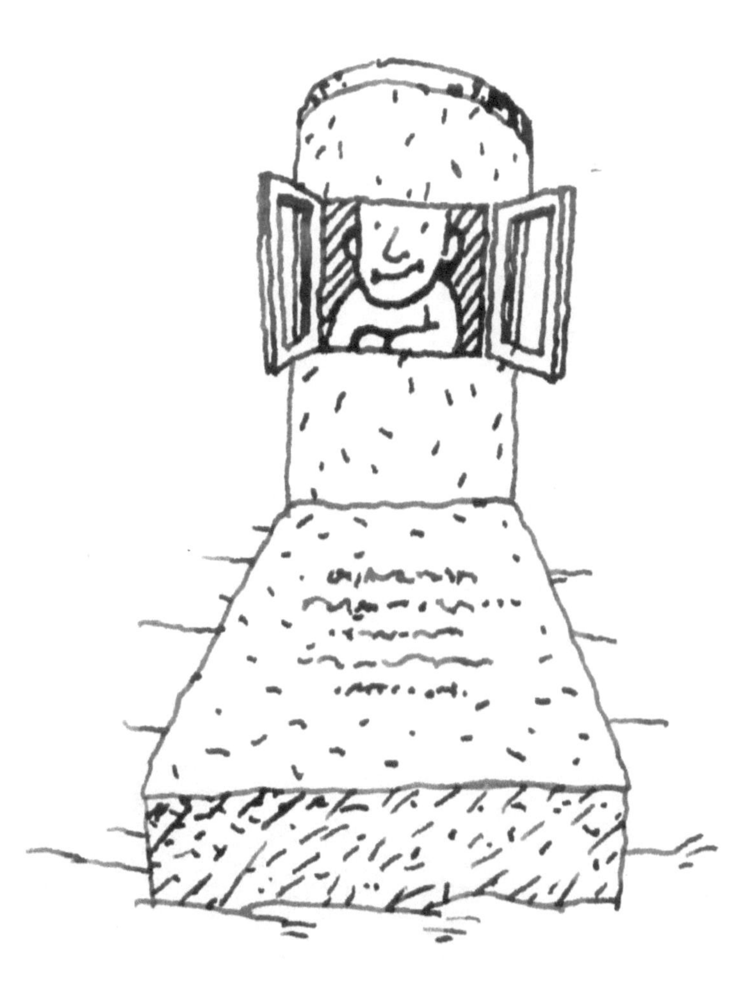

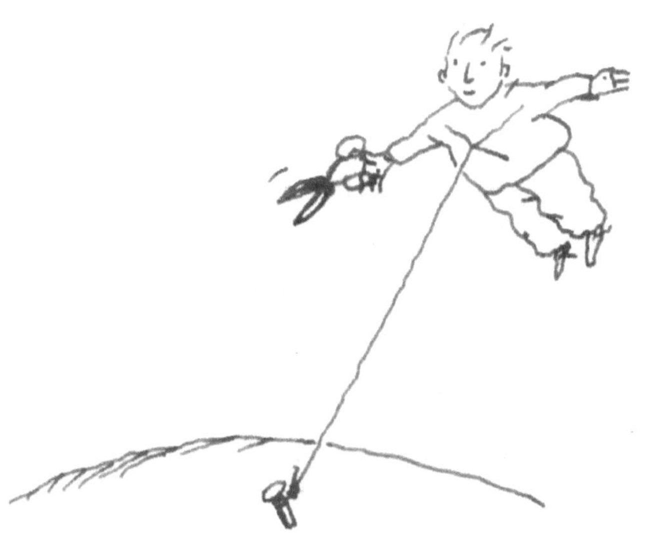

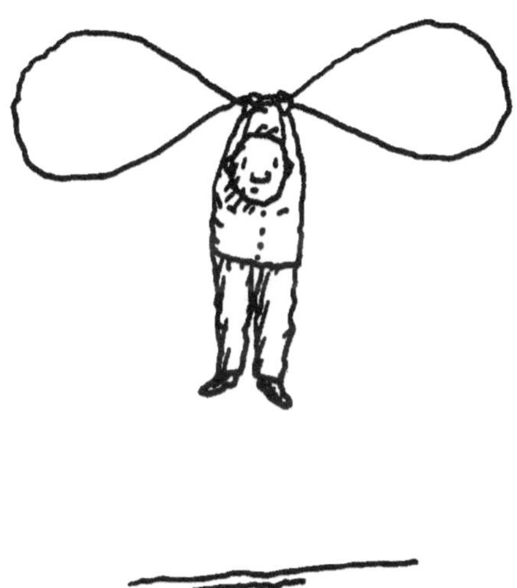

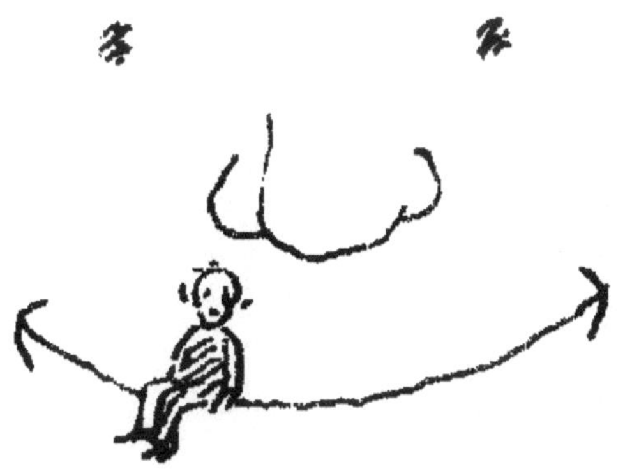

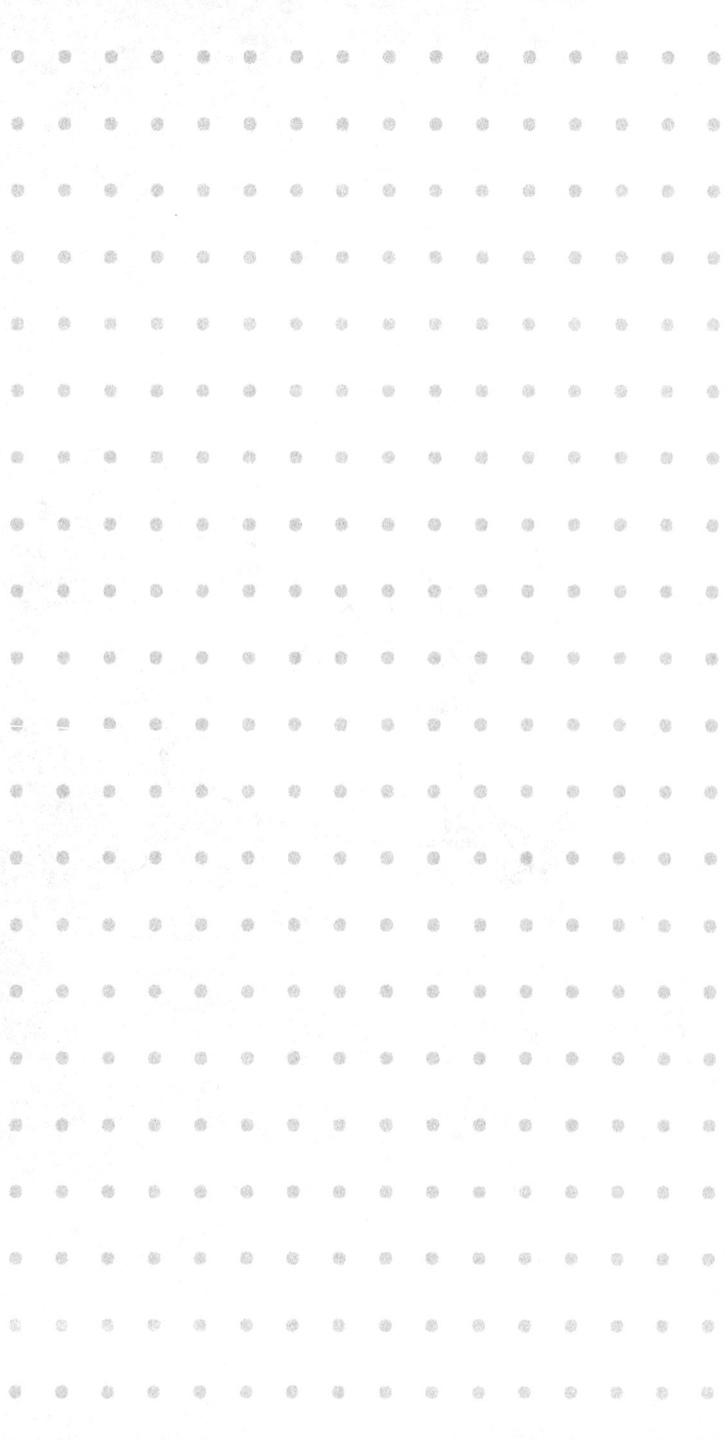

About the author

What difference would it make if you knew the story of my life in my space/time world?